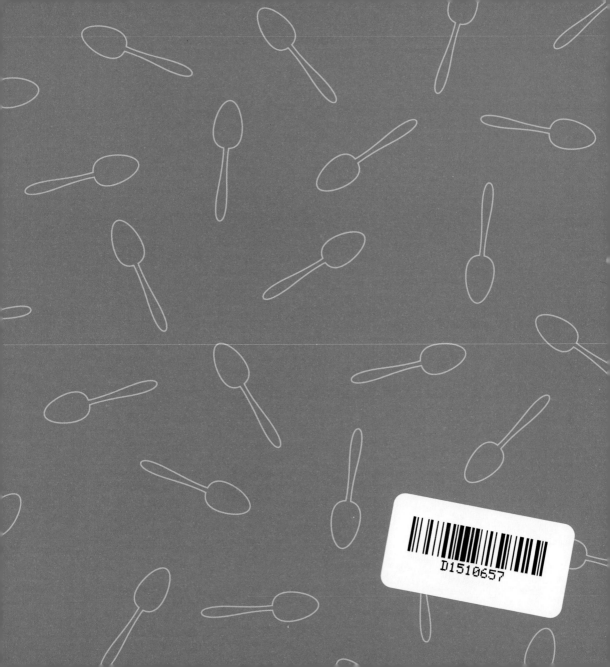

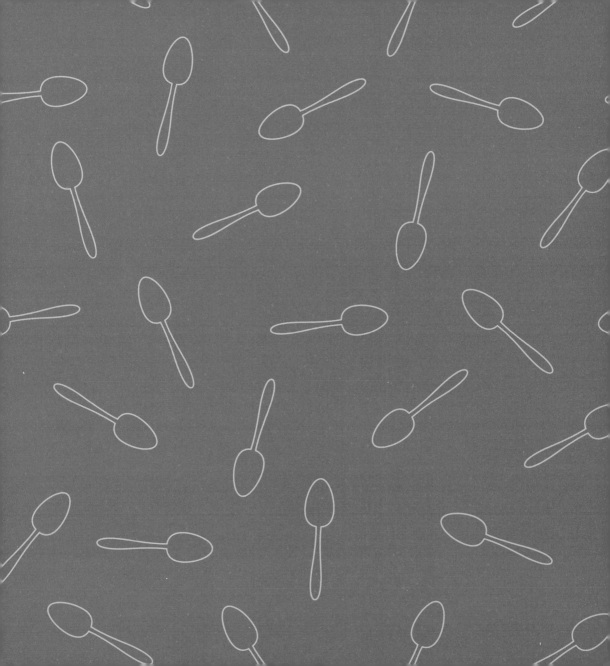

simply soup

simply soup

madge baird

PHOTOGRAPHS BY
lori rice

GIBBS SMITH
TO ENRICH AND INSPIRE HUMANKIND

TO MY COLLEAGUES AND FRIENDS WHO WERE WILLING TO TRY
A VARIETY OF SOUPS AND SAY WHAT THEY THOUGHT

First Edition
21 20 19 18 17   5 4 3 2 1

Text © 2017 Madge Baird
Photographs © 2017 Lori Rice

Published by
Gibbs Smith
P.O. Box 667
Layton, Utah 84041

1.800.835.4993 orders
www.gibbs-smith.com

Designed by Katie Jennings Campbell
Printed and bound in Hong Kong

Gibbs Smith books are printed on either recycled, 100% post-consumer waste, FSC-certified
papers or on paper produced from sustainable PEFC-certified forest/controlled wood source.
Learn more at www.pefc.org.

Library of Congress Control Number: 2017935136
ISBN: 978-1-4236-4787-4

contents

introduction

THERE ARE AS MANY KINDS OF SOUP AND WAYS TO MAKE IT AS THERE ARE PEOPLE ON THE EARTH! At least that's what it seems like to me. Take a simple tomato soup, for instance: you can make it using canned tomatoes or home-jarred goods; or you can step out to the garden (or visit a farmers market) and choose succulent fresh tomatoes to start your soup; different tomato varieties will produce different flavorful results. You can add herbs or spices, hot sauce if you wish, or a little bit of sugar to bring out the tomatoes' natural sweetness. You can add other vegetables and blend them all together, as in my Roasted Ratatouille Soup (page 23) and Red Tomato Gazpacho (page 31). Or you can leave them chunky.

All this is to say that the recipes in *Simply Soup* reflect the way I cook, but they are just starting points for you to develop your own signature soups that your family and friends will gobble down and then sit back and smile over. You can adapt most of these recipes to be vegetarian if that is your preference. You can change the type of meat or use more or less meat than the recipe calls for. I use meat more like a flavoring ingredient in soups, so I tend to use modest amounts cut into small pieces. That doesn't mean you need to. If your household is full of meat eaters, or if you want to use up all of a leftover chicken or roast, don't worry about a couple of cups extra meat in the stew. Just adapt the liquid as you go so the balance between liquid and solids is satisfying to you. I prefer my puréed soups thick; if you like yours thinner than the recipe turns out, increase the amount of liquid at the end, but be sure to taste and rebalance the flavors.

The most important part of soup making is learning how to create a pleasing base, or underlying flavor. What does a teaspoonful of broth taste like on its own? Strive for a pleasant flavor that is neither bland nor salty. The base should support the other ingredients, not overpower them. However, no star ingredient can overcome a flavorless base. Be mindful when adding bouillon, as it is salty. I recommend experimenting with several brands until you determine which ones you like best. Always add in small increments; taste; adjust. Learn to trust your own palate.

A word of warning: time and again I have seen soups grow out of their pots and require subdividing. It starts innocently: *I think I'll put in three potatoes—two doesn't look like enough,* and so on. This is a wonderful thing, because now there is a bounty of delicious soup to share with neighbors! I generally ladle it into quart jars; a quart is about the right amount for two generous meal servings or four restaurant-size servings. I've never had anyone turn down an offer of a quart of soup, and I'll bet you won't either.

I use mostly basic ingredients and basic spices and herbs—everything can be found in a well-stocked supermarket; there is nothing exotic or hard to find. I don't actually measure with spoons or cups. I use the "taste and adjust" method: that is how creativity comes in. There are times when I have finished creating a soup and feel the flavor could benefit from a little something more to make it memorable. I have found that my favorite homemade pesto is that something extra, so I share the recipe with you on page 10. There is something tremendously satisfying about creating a nutritious soup that people enjoy eating.

In times past, making a pot of soup was a way that frugal housewives used up bits of vegetables and meat remaining at the end of a week, rather than letting them spoil or go mushy. I like that idea very much and hope that the recipes here will light a spark in all of us to be more frugal, reduce our food waste, and fill our kitchens with delicious smells of simmering soup or stew. Invite someone over for a bowlful: all you need to add are hunks of bread and some welcoming conversation. These simple soups are for you—and for anyone you care to invite!

basil pesto

Homemade basil pesto is my secret ingredient for "salvaging" soups that need just a little something extra at the end, an enhancement that will take them from mundane to mouthwatering. I use it in vegetable and potato-based soups and meat varieties. To determine whether it would make a good addition to *your* soup, test a tiny bit in a quarter cup of the soup you are making; if you like the flavor, add a tablespoon or two, or more, to the whole pot. Taste and adjust.

MAKES ABOUT 2 PINTS

1½–2 pounds basil leaves
2–3 cloves garlic

⅓–½ cup nuts (raw cashews, pecans, or walnuts)
½–¾ cup finely grated Parmesan cheese

Juice of 1 lemon
Good-quality extra virgin olive oil

Place all ingredients except the olive oil into a food processor or blender. As soon as you begin processing, start pouring in the oil and continue adding until the pesto is a consistency you like. I prefer a tight (spoonable) pesto, without a lot of extra oil; but if you prefer a looser (pourable) pesto, then add more oil. Store pesto in small jars and refrigerate for up to 3 weeks; add a thin film of oil over the top of refrigerated pesto to help retain its color. For longer storage, freeze in jars or as cubes.

starter soups

tomatillo-avocado soup

If you love avocados, you'll love this soup. It is a creamy, palate-pleasing starter dish for a meal of fresh tacos. Enjoy it heated, at room temperature, or chilled.

1 small onion, roughly chopped

1 clove garlic, minced

1 tablespoon vegetable oil

1 pound fresh tomatillos,* husks removed, roughly chopped

1 (14.5-ounce) can chicken broth

1 teaspoon salt

½ teaspoon cumin

¼ teaspoon dried Mexican oregano

2 ripe Hass avocados, flesh removed from skins

½ cup fresh cilantro

1 teaspoon sugar

2 teaspoons lime juice

4 tablespoons heavy cream (optional)*

In a saucepan, sauté the onion and garlic in oil over medium-high heat for 3 minutes. Do not allow to burn. Add the tomatillos, broth, salt, cumin, and oregano. Cover pan and let simmer for 7 to 10 minutes, until tomatillos are soft; remove from heat. Add the avocado, cilantro, sugar, and lime juice. Purée all together until smooth. Taste and adjust seasonings with salt, sugar, or cream. Reheat, or serve at room temperature or chilled.

*Choose some tomatillos that are lighter in color (riper) if you are picking from your garden and have the option. The darkest green ones are a bit too tart for this recipe. Cream will help mellow the tartness.

minty cucumber-melon soup

This cold soup is a refreshing first course for a spring or summer meal. You needn't worry too much about the size of the melon or cucumber: it all works out in the blender.

──────── MAKES 4 TO 6 SMALL SERVINGS ────────

1 medium honeydew melon

1 slicing cucumber

1 tablespoon local honey

6 ounces plain yogurt

1–2 teaspoons chopped mint leaves, plus 4–6 small leaves, for garnish

To prepare the melon, remove and discard the seeds; scoop the flesh into a bowl.

Peel the cucumber and remove the seeds with a spoon. Cut each half into 3 or 4 pieces. Place melon, cucumber, honey, yogurt, and 1 to 2 teaspoons mint leaves in a blender. Process until liquefied and smooth. Chill if desired, or divide among serving bowls and serve at room temperature. Garnish with mint leaves.

tangy ginger peach soup

This recipe uses frozen, but has all the lusciousness of summer-sweet peaches. It makes a lovely meal starter summer through autumn.

1 pound frozen peaches, semi-thawed, or 1 ½ pounds fresh peaches, peeled and pitted

2 ounces goat cheese*

1 ½ teaspoons grated gingerroot

1–2 tablespoons local honey, depending on sweetness of peaches

½ teaspoon chopped cilantro or basil leaves (optional)

Pinch of salt

Place all ingredients in a blender and process until liquefied and smooth. Adjust seasonings with additional sweetener if desired. Serve chilled or at room temperature.

*Cream cheese is a wonderful substitute if you want a smooth, non-tangy, flavor.

VARIATION: For Nectarine Soup, substitute ripe nectarines for peaches. You do not need to peel, just pit the nectarines.

beet and apple soup

I love the earthy flavor of beets all by themselves, but apples brighten their flavor in this recipe. To adapt the color of the soup to your liking, add extra liquid from the beets. The addition of cream changes it to a deep rose color. Choose your bowls accordingly!

1 tablespoon olive oil

1 teaspoon butter

2 cooking apples, peeled and thinly sliced

1 carrot, peeled and thinly sliced

1 rib celery, thinly sliced

2 (14-ounce) cans beets, liquid reserved, or 2 pounds fresh beets, boiled and skins removed

1 cup apple juice

1 (14.5-ounce) can vegetable broth

1 bay leaf

$\frac{1}{2}$ teaspoon salt

$\frac{1}{4}$ teaspoon pepper

Vegetable bouillon (optional)

$\frac{1}{4}$ cup heavy whipping cream (optional)

Heat oil and butter in a medium saucepan. Place apples, carrot, and celery in pan and cook, covered, over medium heat until apples are softened, stirring frequently to prevent the butter from burning. Add beets, apple juice, broth, bay leaf, salt, and pepper to the pan. Bring to a low boil and cook, covered, for about 20 minutes while vegetables soften. Discard bay leaf.

Purée the soup to a smooth consistency. Heat through and taste; adjust seasoning with $\frac{1}{2}$ teaspoon vegetable bouillon if desired. Adjust the color with additions of reserved beet liquid. Cream can be added to mellow the flavor if desired.

creamy parsnip and apple soup

If parsnips haven't been in your vegetable repertoire, this is a fun way to try them. The sweetness of the parsnips and apples work well together, and the dairy products mellow the soup to a smooth, appealing blend. It's yummy reheated for lunch the next day.

1 small onion, chopped

2 tablespoons butter

2 tablespoons olive oil

2 tart-sweet apples, peeled and chopped

1 $\frac{1}{4}$ pounds parsnips, peeled and chopped

3 cups water

1 tablespoon chicken bouillon powder or base

1 tablespoon lemon juice

1 teaspoon salt

$\frac{1}{2}$ teaspoon cinnamon

$\frac{1}{2}$ teaspoon nutmeg

1 cup whipping cream

1 cup milk

1 tablespoon cornstarch mixed with 2 tablespoons water (optional)

In a large saucepan, sauté the onion in butter and oil over medium heat for 3 minutes. Add apples and sauté 3 to 4 minutes more. Add the parsnips, water, bouillon, lemon juice, salt, cinnamon, and nutmeg. Cover and bring to a boil; reduce heat and simmer for 20 minutes, until parsnips are tender. Let cool a little, and then purée the soup and return to pan, adding cream and milk. Heat to just boiling, stirring frequently. If soup is too thin, thicken with cornstarch slurry; soup must be bubbling for the cornstarch to do its work.

swiss cheese and cider soup

This is one of my favorite soups to serve as a starter to a nice meal. Its sweetness offers a surprising first taste. The flavor is sophisticated and the texture creamy. Sparkling cider gives it a little extra zing. Your dinner guests will wish they could have seconds.

⅓ cup finely chopped onion

1 small sweet apple, peeled, cored, and grated (about 1 cup)

2 tablespoons butter

2 tablespoons all-purpose flour

⅔ cup apple cider, sparkling or still

⅔ cup half-and-half

¼ teaspoon nutmeg

1 cup grated Swiss Emmentaler cheese

⅛ teaspoon salt

¼ teaspoon pepper

In a medium pan, sauté onion and apple in butter over medium heat until soft. Stir in the flour. Add apple cider and stir or whisk to create a thin sauce surrounding the chunks. Add the half-and-half and nutmeg. Using a hand-held blender, purée to desired consistency right in the pot (a slight amount of texture is perfectly agreeable). If you use a stand blender, purée in batches; then return to the pan.

Stir soup over medium heat until hot. Add the cheese in three parts, stirring after each addition until melted. Season with salt and pepper.

roasted red pepper soup

Sophisticated flavor—mild with a hint of sweetness—makes this soup ideally suited to start a company dinner. Alternatively, it makes an excellent dipping sauce for grilled cheese sandwiches. If you don't have time to char your own peppers, roasted red peppers from a jar taste just fine.

3 red bell peppers, roasted and skin removed*

6 ripe plum tomatoes, quartered

½ cup water

2 tablespoons lemon juice

½ cube Knorr vegetable bouillon

Pinch of crushed red pepper flakes

Pinch of black pepper

½ cup heavy cream

Place the peppers, tomatoes, water, lemon juice, bouillon, pepper flakes, and pepper in a saucepan and bring to a boil, stirring. Reduce heat to a simmer and cook for 3 to 4 minutes while tomatoes break down. Transfer tomato mixture to a blender or food processor and purée. Return to the saucepan and add cream; heat through.

*Roast peppers over the flame of a gas stove, on the grill, or under the broiler until the skin is charred all over. Wrap peppers in wet paper towels or in a sealed plastic bag and let cool. When cool, remove stems and seeds, and then gently scrape off the charred skin with a spoon.

essentially vegetables

roasted ratatouille soup

Roasting all the vegetables together in the oven is the easiest way to get them cooked. This way you don't have to tend them or adjust the heat up and down on the stove. In the end, they will all be puréed together. The eggplant has a mellowing effect on the tomatoes and provides a bit of creaminess to the texture.

──────── MAKES 6 TO 8 SERVINGS ────────

6 red-ripe tomatoes
2 zucchini
2 Japanese eggplants
2 onions, peeled

2 bell peppers, any color
2 cloves garlic, sliced
4 tablespoons extra virgin olive oil

Salt and pepper
½ cup chopped fresh basil, or 2 teaspoons dried basil

Preheat oven to 425 degrees F.

Cut all the vegetables into chunks and place in a large bowl. Pour olive oil over vegetables, season with salt and pepper, and then toss to coat. Transfer vegetables to a roasting pan. Bake, covered, for 30 minutes and then uncovered, for 15 more minutes, or until all vegetables are cooked and some have brown edges. Turn vegetables at least twice during cooking time.

Purée vegetables in batches, with a sprinkling of basil, to the degree of smoothness you like. Mix batches together in a large pot and reheat. Adjust seasonings with salt and pepper to taste. Serve hot.

fresh tomato soup

This is the best! Don't be afraid to mix yellow tomatoes with reds, or sweet cherry tomatoes with slicers. Blending varieties makes a more interesting flavor, and it will be oh, so slightly different each time you make it.

——————— MAKES 6 TO 8 SERVINGS ———————

2 pounds ripe tomatoes
  (any red, yellow, or
  orange varieties)
1 tablespoon olive oil
¾ cup chopped onion

½ cup water
1 teaspoon Better Than
  Bouillon chicken base
Pinch of garlic powder

½ teaspoon sugar
Salt
Freshly snipped chives, for
  garnish

Immerse washed tomatoes in a medium soup pot of boiling water for 1 to 1½ minutes. Transfer tomatoes to a colander and discard the hot water. Let tomatoes cool.

While tomatoes are cooling, rinse the pot thoroughly and return it to the stove. Add oil and heat on medium high. Sauté the onion until it turns translucent. Remove pot from the heat.

Remove and discard the skins, tough cores, and as many seeds as possible from the tomatoes. Crush tomatoes with your hands over the soup pot and add them to the onion. Add the water, bouillon, garlic powder, and sugar. Bring to a slow boil over medium heat, stirring frequently. Simmer soup for 5 to 8 minutes, and then add salt to taste. Remove from heat. Serve the soup as is, or puréed. Garnish with chives.

VARIATIONS: For Tomato Soup with Boursin, add ½ cup roughly chopped basil leaves and 6 ounces Boursin Garlic & Fine Herbs cheese before puréeing; omit the chives.

For Simple Cream of Tomato Soup, purée the soup and stir in 1 cup heavy whipping cream while reheating.

three sisters soup

There are various tellings of the Native American legend about how corn, squash, and climbing beans make companionable crops, virtually growing together, supporting each other: corn stands tall and provides shade for squash and a pole for beans to climb on. True or not, the three sister ingredients combine for a delicious soup.

MAKES 6 TO 8 SERVINGS

1 onion, chopped

1 red bell pepper, finely chopped

2 tablespoons vegetable oil

1–2 cloves garlic, minced

4 cups puréed winter squash (such as butternut, Hubbard, banana, etc.)

2 cups water

2 Knorr chicken bouillon cubes, or 1 1/2 tablespoons bouillon powder or base

2 teaspoons cumin

1/2 teaspoon cayenne pepper

2 (14.5-ounce) cans cut green beans, drained and rinsed

1 (14-ounce) bag frozen corn, thawed

2 cups half-and-half

1/2 bunch fresh cilantro, chopped

In a large saucepan, sauté the onion and bell pepper in oil for 3 to 4 minutes, until onion begins to turn translucent. Add the garlic and sauté for 3 minutes more, stirring. Add the squash, water, bouillon, cumin, and cayenne; mix well. Cover and bring to a boil, stirring frequently; reduce heat and simmer for 8 to 10 minutes. Add green beans and corn and simmer for 5 minutes, stirring. Stir in half-and-half and cilantro and heat through.

vegetarian minestrone

Making a batch of minestrone is a smart and tasty way to use up extra vegetables. Almost any type can be included. Or use canned vegetables to supplement the fresh ones. With or without pasta is the cook's choice.

1 small onion, chopped

1/2 cup chopped celery

1/2 cup chopped carrots

2 tablespoons vegetable oil

1 1/2 cups thinly sliced cabbage

2 cups hot water, plus more

3/4 cup chopped fresh herbs (such as basil, oregano, and thyme) or 2 teaspoons dried herbs

1/2 teaspoon garlic powder

2 (14.5-ounce) cans diced tomatoes, with liquid

1 cup cut green beans

1 (15-ounce) can garbanzo beans, drained and rinsed

1 small zucchini, halved and sliced

1 yellow summer squash, halved and sliced (optional)

2 large handfuls spinach leaves

3/4 cup small shell or tube pasta or orzo (optional)

Salt and pepper

Vegetable bouillon (optional)

Grated Parmesan cheese, for garnish

In a large soup pot, cook the onion, celery, and carrots in hot oil for about 5 minutes, stirring twice. Add the cabbage and 2 cups hot water. Cover with a lid, raise heat to medium high and bring to a boil; then reduce to a low boil and cook for about 10 minutes to let cabbage soften.

Stir in the herbs and garlic powder. Add the tomatoes, beans, zucchini, yellow squash, spinach and enough hot water to cover all the vegetables. Cover and bring to a boil again, and then reduce to a low boil. Cook, covered, for about 15 minutes while the vegetables flavor the broth. Add optional pasta and cook for about 8 minutes. Be sure there is enough water to cook the pasta. When pasta is cooked, taste and adjust seasonings with salt, pepper, additional herbs, and vegetable bouillon. Garnish individual bowls with Parmesan.

red tomato gazpacho

An ultra-refreshing cold summer soup, this recipe is best when made with very ripe garden-grown or farmers market tomatoes.

MAKES 12 TO 15 SERVINGS

5 pounds red tomatoes, peeled

2 cucumbers, peeled and sliced

1 large green bell pepper, seeded and sliced

1 red onion, peeled and quartered

2 large cloves garlic, minced

1 bunch cilantro, thick stems discarded

1/4 cup red wine vinegar

1/4 cup olive oil

Juice of 1 lime

32 ounces tomato juice

Salt and pepper

Grated Parmesan cheese, for garnish

Croutons, for garnish

Using a food processor, process the tomatoes, cucumbers, bell pepper, onion, and garlic in batches to desired consistency. Pour into a large bowl and stir in the cilantro, vinegar, olive oil, lime juice, and tomato juice; season to taste with salt and pepper. Ladle into cups or bowls and garnish with Parmesan and croutons.

V8 soup with rotini

This soup can be made in about 30 minutes on the stove. If you prefer to slow cook it, add the precooked pasta about a half hour before serving. This recipe is inspired by one that my friend Robin McLellen makes.

————— MAKES ABOUT 8 SERVINGS —————

1 (14.5-ounce) can Italian-style diced tomatoes

1 (8-ounce) can tomato sauce

3 cups V8 vegetable juice

1 (15-ounce) can vegetable broth, plus 1 can water

1 ½ teaspoons dried basil

1 teaspoon dried oregano

½ teaspoon pepper

½ teaspoon chili powder

2 cups rotini pasta

1 (15-ounce) can red beans drained

1 cup frozen corn

1 cup frozen green beans

1 cup frozen carrots

¼ cup roughly chopped fresh parsley, for garnish

In a large soup pot, bring the tomatoes, tomato sauce, juice, broth and water, basil, oregano, pepper, and chili powder to a boil. Reduce heat and simmer for about 15 minutes. Cook the pasta in a pot of boiling water for 5 to 7 minutes. Drain and set aside.

Meanwhile, add the beans and frozen vegetables to the soup and bring to a low boil for about 5 minutes while vegetables cook. Stir in the cooked pasta and let the soup simmer for another 7 to 10 minutes while flavors meld. Garnish bowls of soup with a sprinkle of chopped parsley.

For a slow cooker option, place the tomatoes, tomato sauce, juice, broth and water, basil, oregano, pepper, and chili powder in a slow cooker on low setting for 4 to 10 hours. Add the frozen vegetables about 1 hour before you plan to serve; increase heat to high. Or cook vegetables separately before adding. Cook the pasta separately and add to the soup within 15 minutes of serving.

VARIATION: For V8 with Meatballs and Rotini, add about 1 pound frozen Italian-style meatballs to the slow cooker at least 1 hour before serving, and turn heat to high. If on the stovetop add the meatballs 10 minutes before vegetables.

kale minestrone

This satisfying soup tastes even better on days two and three, if it lasts that long. The spiciness of the canned tomatoes stands up to a necessary small addition of water when reheating, as the pasta continues to absorb a bit of liquid.

1 medium onion, chopped

1–2 cloves garlic, minced

1 tablespoon olive oil

1 bunch Lacinato kale, thickest stems removed

4–5 leaves curly kale, thickest stems removed

1 (14.5-ounce) can Mexican-style stewed tomatoes, chopped, with their juice

3 cubes Knorr vegetable bouillon

3–4 cups water

1 tablespoon Worcestershire sauce

1 tablespoon chopped fresh basil

1 1/2 teaspoons dried oregano

1/2 teaspoon pepper

5 carrots, peeled and sliced

1 (15-ounce) can garbanzo beans, drained

3/4 cup ditalini pasta

Salt

In a large pot, cook the onion and garlic in the oil for about 3 minutes; stirring frequently. Meanwhile, roughly chop the kale.

Add the tomatoes, bouillon, water, Worcestershire sauce, and chopped kale to the pot. Bring to a boil and add the basil, oregano, and pepper. Cover and simmer about 20 minutes to cook the kale completely. Add the carrots and beans and cook until softened. Stir in the pasta and add more water if needed. Cook until pasta is tender. Add more water if needed. Adjust seasoning with salt to taste.

roasted cauliflower soup

Roasting the cauliflower gives this soup a rustic flavor, so it is essential to remove the cauliflower from the oven before it gets mushy. Adding sautéed mushrooms as a variation enhances the earthy flavor.

1 small to medium-size cauliflower

¼ cup olive oil

1 ½ cups water

1 tablespoon chicken bouillon powder or base

½ teaspoon paprika

1 teaspoon dried thyme leaves

2 teaspoons dehydrated chopped onion

⅓ cup chopped pecans

½–1 cup milk or whipping cream (as needed to thin)

½–⅔ cup grated Parmesan cheese

2 tablespoons butter (optional)

2 tablespoons all-purpose flour (optional)

1 tablespoon dried parsley

Preheat oven to 400 degrees F. Remove leaves from the cauliflower and break it into florets, or slice it crosswise about 1 inch thick. Toss cauliflower in the olive oil, and then spread it in a single layer on a baking sheet. Roast for 30 to 35 minutes, until a fork can easily pierce the cauliflower. Note: Some caramelization will enhance the flavor, but turn the cauliflower over with a spatula once during roasting to prevent burning.

Remove cauliflower from oven and transfer to a pot with the water. Add the bouillon, paprika, thyme, and onion. Cover and heat to boiling. Remove from heat, add the pecans and milk. Purée soup to desired consistency. Add the cheese and stir to melt. If the soup is too thin, make a roux with the butter and flour; stir roux into the soup. Bring to a simmer and stir constantly while it thickens. Add the parsley. Adjust flavor and thickness with additional bouillon and milk if desired.

VARIATION: To make a heartier White Bean with Cauliflower Soup, add 1 (15-ounce) can great Northern or cannellini beans, drained and rinsed, before or after puréeing, plus 1 cup chopped mushrooms and 2 tablespoons chopped parsley sautéed together in butter.

broccoli cheese soup

Broccoli cheese is an American soup classic and there are scores of recipes for it. My neighbor told me she couldn't resist this version: she ate a whole quart in one sitting!

MAKES ABOUT 2 QUARTS

1 bunch broccoli

4 cups chicken broth

1 cup water

2 tablespoons dehydrated chopped onion

1 tablespoon Knorr chicken bouillon powder or Better Than Bouillon chicken base

$\frac{1}{8}$ teaspoon garlic powder

1 cup half-and-half

1 cup whipping cream

3 cups grated medium cheddar cheese

3 tablespoons cornstarch mixed with 3 tablespoons water (optional)

$\frac{1}{4}$ teaspoon turmeric (optional)

Salt and pepper

Chopped fresh chives or parsley, for garnish

Cut broccoli heads into florets. Remove and discard the toughest part of the stems and peel the rest. Cut stems into small pieces.

In a large covered saucepan, bring the broth, water, onion, bouillon, garlic powder, and broccoli to a low boil. Cook until the broccoli is tender but not mushy, 7 to 8 minutes. Purée broccoli with the liquid to desired consistency.

Reheat broccoli purée and add the half-and-half and cream; bring to a low boil. When hot, stir in the cheese 1 cup at a time until melted. Stir half of the cornstarch mixture into lightly bubbling soup to thicken, whisking constantly. Add the remaining cornstarch mixture if desired. Add the turmeric if you want to boost the color. Season to taste with salt and pepper. Garnish bowls of soup with chives or parsley.

VARIATION: For Pumped-Up Broccoli Cheese, 1 grated carrot and 1 $\frac{1}{2}$ cups shredded cooked chicken are hearty additions.

southwest pumpkin stew

If you've tried pumpkin soup before and didn't care for it, I think you'll feel differently about this recipe. It's hearty and satisfying. Apple adds a surprising sweet factor; choose any variety that you would use in a pie.

─────── MAKES 12 TO 15 SERVINGS ───────

2 tablespoons oil
1 onion, chopped
3 ribs celery, chopped
3 carrots, diced
2–3 golden delicious apples, chopped with skin on
2 (15-ounce) cans pumpkin purée

1 (14.5-ounce) can chicken broth
1 (15-ounce) can black beans, drained and rinsed
2 (15-ounce) cans corn, drained
2–3 cups diced cooked chicken
2 teaspoons cumin*

2 teaspoons dried parsley or cilantro
2 teaspoons salt
1/2 teaspoon pepper
1–2 Knorr chicken bouillon cubes, powder, or base (optional)

In a large soup pot, heat the oil over medium heat. Sauté the onion, celery, carrots, and apples for about 15 minutes, or until onion is translucent, stirring frequently.

Raise heat to medium high and stir in the pumpkin and broth; bring to a low boil, stirring occasionally. Add the beans, corn, chicken, cumin, parsley, salt, pepper, and bouillon; bring soup back to boiling, stirring occasionally. Reduce heat to low and continue simmering, covered, for about 45 minutes while the flavors meld. Stir occasionally. Taste and adjust flavor as desired. If too thick, add a small amount of water.

*Don't care for the flavor of cumin? Omit it and replace with half as much chili powder or a little cinnamon or nutmeg. Be careful not to over-spice.

african peanut soup

This vegetarian soup has a secret ingredient: peanut butter! It's the finishing touch that turns the soup into a creamy delight. Be careful about overdoing the gingerroot; its pronounced flavor can overpower and add more burn than you intend.

─────── MAKES 12 TO 15 SERVINGS ───────

3 tablespoons peanut or vegetable oil

2 cups chopped onion

2 teaspoons red chile flakes

2 pounds carrots, peeled and quartered

2 large sweet potatoes (about 2 pounds), peeled and cubed

2 (14-ounce) cans vegetable broth

4 cups tomato juice

1 tablespoon grated fresh gingerroot

1 ½ cups peanut butter, creamy or chunky

Hot sauce

Chopped peanuts, for garnish

Heat oil in a large soup pot over medium-high heat. Sauté onion and chile flakes until onion becomes translucent. Add carrots, sweet potatoes, and broth plus just enough water to cover the vegetables.

Cover and bring to a boil; cook until vegetables are tender, 20 to 25 minutes. Stir tomato juice and gingerroot into the vegetables.

Using a hand-held blender, purée soup to a smooth consistency right in the pot. If you use a stand blender, purée in batches.

Heat the purée and stir in peanut butter. Season to taste with hot sauce (the soup should offer a mild bite but not a sting). Serve hot garnished with chopped peanuts.

butternut soup
with apple and rosemary

Perfect for autumn, this soup has a pretty color and delightful flavor. It makes a lovely starter for a company meal.

——————— MAKES 4 TO 6 SERVINGS ———————

1 tart apple, peeled and chopped

½ small onion, chopped

3 tablespoons butter

1 tablespoon Knorr chicken bouillon, plus more for seasoning

3 cups water

½ teaspoon finely chopped fresh rosemary

1 slice wheat bread, torn

½ large butternut squash, seeded, peeled, and diced

½ cup whipping cream

Milk or water (optional)

Salt and pepper

Chopped fresh parsley, for garnish (optional)

Thin apple slices, skin on, or crushed dried apple, for garnish (optional)

In a medium saucepan, sauté the apple and onion in butter for 4 to 5 minutes, stirring frequently. Add the bouillon, water, rosemary, bread, and squash. Bring to a low boil and cook for 15 minutes, or until the squash is tender. Remove from heat and let cool a little.

Purée soup to a smooth consistency right in the pot using a hand-held blender. Or, if using a stand blender, purée in batches. Add cream and blend until smooth. Thin with a little milk or water if desired. Return soup to heat until warmed through. Adjust seasoning with bouillon, salt, and pepper to taste. Garnish as desired with parsley and apple.

easy tomato basil soup

Who doesn't love tomato basil? Canned tomatoes make this a convenient, anytime soup. Craving a grilled cheese sandwich? See the variation below to turn this into a fabulous grilled cheese dipping sauce.

1 small onion, sliced

1–2 tablespoons olive oil

2 (15-ounce) cans stewed or crushed tomatoes, with juice

2 tablespoons chopped fresh basil, or $\frac{1}{2}$ teaspoon dried basil

1 teaspoon sugar

1 cup tomato juice, divided

Salt and pepper

Croutons (optional)

Chopped parsley (optional)

Shredded or shaved Parmesan cheese (optional)

In a medium frying pan, sauté the onion in oil then blend to liquefy. Add the tomatoes, basil, and sugar. Add $\frac{1}{2}$ cup tomato juice and blend, stopping to add more juice if the mixture is too thick for the blender to process. Reheat the soup, adding any tomato juice that remains. Season with salt and pepper to taste. Garnish with croutons, parsley, and Parmesan if desired.

VARIATION: For a great Grilled Cheese Sandwich Dip, temper $\frac{1}{2}$ cup heavy cream by stirring in $\frac{1}{4}$ cup of the hot tomato soup. (Be sure to use heavy cream: it is more stable and will not curdle as whipping cream might.) Then stir the tempered cream into the soup and combine well.

harvest moon soup

The choice of vegetables is up to the cook. I use whatever vegetables are available at the end of the summer harvest season, as fall crops come on. If you select broccoli, add it to the soup pot late in the cooking so it doesn't turn mushy.

1 onion, chopped
2–3 cloves garlic, minced
2 tablespoons olive oil
2 tablespoons butter
1 cup chopped fresh herbs (such as basil, oregano, dill, rosemary, and/or mint)

1 bay leaf
8 cups chopped fresh vegetables (such as tomatoes, corn, summer squash, turnips, carrots, peppers, broccoli, cabbage, and/or greens)
3 cups chicken broth*

3 cups vegetable broth*
Salt and pepper
Grated Parmesan cheese, for garnish

In a large soup pot, sauté the onion and garlic in oil and butter for 4 to 5 minutes. Add the fresh herbs and sauté for 1 minute more. Add the bay leaf, vegetables, and broths. Cover pot and bring soup to a boil; cook for 20 to 25 minutes, until vegetables are fork-tender. Taste and adjust seasonings with salt and pepper. Serve garnished with cheese if desired.

*You can substitute 6 cups water plus 6 small or 3 large chicken or vegetable bouillon cubes.

easy french onion soup

This is an easy version of an age-old classic. If you want to be more authentic, ladle soup into individual ovenproof bowls and top with a slice of Gruyère or Swiss cheese. Be sure to place bowls on a baking sheet in the oven to protect from spillovers.

——————— MAKES 4 SERVINGS ———————

3–4 medium yellow onions, halved and sliced

2 tablespoons olive oil

1 tablespoon butter

2 cups chicken broth

1 cup water

2 teaspoons beef base

$\frac{1}{4}$ teaspoon ground marjoram

Seasoned croutons

4 slices Swiss or Gruyère cheese

In a medium saucepan, sauté the onions in oil and butter over medium-low heat for 25 to 30 minutes, stirring frequently, until they caramelize. Add the broth, water, beef base, and marjoram; cover pan and simmer soup for 20 minutes while flavors meld.

To serve, drop 3 or 4 seasoned croutons into the bottom of each ovenproof bowl. Ladle hot soup over the croutons and top with cheese. Place bowls on a baking sheet and put under the broiler for about 2 minutes while the cheese melts and gets a little brown on top.

asian hot pot

Sitting around a table with friends, cooking your own food in a shared pot of simmering broth is an intimate experience. At home, you can use a hot plate to keep the broth lightly simmering. Or you can achieve a similar result (without all the elbows) by cooking the meat and vegetables quickly in small batches on the stove. Using chopsticks makes the soup even tastier and a whole lot of fun!

———— MAKES 6 TO 8 SERVINGS ————

DIPPING SAUCE

3 tablespoons soy sauce

2 teaspoons sesame oil

2 teaspoons brown sugar

2 teaspoons water

1/2 teaspoon rice vinegar

Dash of hot sauce
  (optional)

NOODLES

4–8 ounces cellophane
  noodles or Chinese rice
  noodles

STIR-INS

2 pounds very thinly
  sliced* meat, chicken,
  fish, or raw shrimp

2–2 1/2 pounds vegetables
  sliced or cut into bite-
  size pieces (e.g., napa or
  savoy cabbage, baby bok
  choy, mushrooms, bean
  sprouts, very thin slices
  sweet potato or carrot)

16 ounce package firm
  tofu, drained, cut into
  1/2-inch squares

BROTH

8 cups chicken stock

1/3 cup soy sauce

3 scallions, chopped, white
  and green parts

2 cloves garlic, finely
  minced

1 1/2 tablespoons finely
  grated fresh gingerroot

1 tablespoon sesame oil

DIPPING SAUCE

In a small saucepan, bring all the dipping sauce ingredients to a simmer over medium heat. Stir well and remove from heat. Use small bowls to divide the sauce into 6 to 8 individual portions.

*Freeze chicken, beef, and pork for 30 minutes to make slicing easier or have your butcher do the slicing for you.

>> continued

NOODLES

Prepare the noodles according to package directions. Drain and then cut with scissors as needed to divide among individual serving bowls.

STIR-INS

Arrange the prepared meats and vegetables in overlapping rows on a tray for easy selection.

BROTH

Place all the ingredients in a saucepan on the stove and bring to a low boil. Ladle about $\frac{1}{2}$ cup broth over the noodles in each bowl. If you will be cooking the food in a hot pot at the table, now is the time to transfer the remaining broth to the pot you will use for communal cooking; bring it to a simmer.

TO FINISH

Allow guests to choose their own meats and vegetables. Using chopsticks or other suitable utensils, each person can transfer their selections to the broth one or two pieces at a time and then to their bowls immediately after cooking. Because the slices are thin, the meat and vegetables will cook quickly (from 30 to 60 seconds) in constantly simmering broth.

Keep your eye on the temperature of the broth throughout the meal and adjust it up or down to keep it as constant as possible at a low simmer. People will continue cooking pieces of food and moving those to their bowls throughout the meal.

Serve dipping sauce on the side.

pots of potatoes

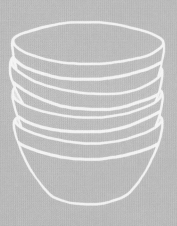

zuppa toscana

This is a scrumptious way to enhance potato soup. Some people can take the heat, but if you can't, stick with mild Italian sausage.

1 large onion, diced

1 ½ pounds mild Italian ground sausage*

6–7 large red potatoes, peeled, quartered, and thinly sliced

2 (14.5-ounce) cans chicken broth

4 cups water

1–2 teaspoons red chile flakes

1 pint whipping cream

1 bunch kale, tough stems removed and leaves chopped

Chicken bouillon powder or base (optional)

In a large soup pot, brown the onion and sausage; drain fat. Add the potatoes, broth, water, and chile flakes. Cover pot and bring to a boil for about 20 minutes, until potatoes are tender.

Stir in the cream. Soup will thicken the longer you keep it warm and stirred. Mix kale into hot soup for about the last 5 minutes of cooking. Taste and adjust seasoning with small addition of bouillon if desired.

*Italian ground turkey can be substituted.

poor man's soup

Every home cook needs to have potato soup in their repertoire. This one is very basic and a good base to build from if you want to add more ingredients.

2 tablespoons oil

1 onion, chopped

3 large baking potatoes, diced

Water

2 tablespoons butter

1 cup milk

1–2 teaspoons salt

$\frac{1}{2}$ teaspoon pepper

In a saucepan, heat the oil over medium high and sauté the onion for about 4 minutes, until it turns translucent. Add the potatoes and enough hot tap water to almost cover. Fit a lid on the pan and bring to a low boil. Cook for 25 to 30 minutes, until potatoes are cooked and the water begins to thicken. Stir frequently to prevent scorching. When potatoes are done, add butter and milk. Heat through. Taste and add salt and pepper.

VARIATIONS: For Rich Man's Potato Soup, dress up the above recipe with additions of protein, cheese, vegetables, or even home-style noodles.

For Roasted Garlic Potato Soup, add 1 to 2 tablespoons chopped roasted garlic from the deli condiment bar.

loaded baked potato soup

Using precooked ingredients lets you whip this up in the microwave in no time at all. Delish!

—————— MAKES 4 SERVINGS ——————

2 baked russet potatoes,
   diced with peel

4 tablespoons sour cream

1 tablespoon bacon grease

1 cup half-and-half

¾ cup grated cheddar or
   Colby Jack cheese

1 tablespoon butter

2 strips crispy-cooked
   bacon, crumbled

Salt and pepper

1 tablespoon chopped fresh
   chives, for garnish

Place the potatoes, sour cream, bacon grease, and half-and-half in a microwave-safe bowl. Cover bowl and microwave on 80 percent power for 3 minutes. Remove bowl and add the cheese, butter, and bacon. Season with salt and pepper to taste; mix together. Cover bowl and microwave on full power for 3 minutes. Remove carefully and mix ingredients again. Serve garnished with chives.

german potato soup

With the soul-satisfying flavor of bacon and a little bit of tartness from the vinegar, this German-style variation on potato soup is a flavorful option to standard potato soups.

6–8 Yukon gold potatoes, peeled and cubed

1 onion, diced

4–5 cups water (enough to cover potatoes)

½ pound bacon, sliced crosswise into thin strips

4 rounded tablespoons all-purpose flour

¾ cup sour cream

2 cups chicken broth

2 cups milk, divided

2 tablespoons white vinegar

1 tablespoon chicken bouillon powder or base

1 teaspoon celery seed

Salt and pepper

4 hard-boiled eggs, chopped, for garnish

Chopped pimento, for garnish

In a large saucepan, boil the potatoes and onion in water until tender; drain.

Meanwhile, cook bacon over medium heat in another large covered saucepan until browned. Drain off all but about ¼ cup of the fat. Stir flour into the bacon and fat and cook on low heat for 2 to 3 minutes. Stir in the sour cream and then the chicken broth to make a thin roux.

Add potatoes and onions to the bacon mixture and fold together. Add 1 cup milk and mix well. Add the vinegar, bouillon, celery seed, and season with salt and pepper to taste. Adjust thickness as desired with the remaining 1 cup milk. Heat and serve with a garnish of eggs and pimento.

kielbasa and potato soup

The smoky sausage creates a flavor that stands up to a hungry-man appetite. A rustic dark rye bread makes a hearty accompaniment.

—————— MAKES 6 SERVINGS ——————

2 tablespoons oil

1 pound kielbasa sausage, cut into ½-inch-thick slices

1 onion, chopped

2 ribs celery, chopped

3 large carrots, sliced

1¼ cups chopped green cabbage

1 bay leaf

1 teaspoon dried basil

1 (14.5-ounce) can beef broth

1 (14.5-ounce) can chicken broth

1 cup water

4 Yukon gold potatoes, peeled and diced

Salt and pepper

In a large saucepan, heat the oil and cook the sausage, onion, celery, carrots, cabbage, and herbs for about 5 minutes. Add the beef broth, chicken broth, and water. Bring to a low boil and cook for about 30 minutes, covered, to develop the flavor.

Add the potatoes and enough hot water to cover, if necessary. Bring to a low boil and cook, covered, until potatoes are done, about 20 to 25 minutes. Season to taste with salt and pepper.

corn chowder with ham and pesto

This is a yummy, filling soup that doesn't take very long to make. The pesto makes it unique, as does a small amount of bell pepper. Since the bouillon and ham both contain salt, no other salt is needed.

MAKES ABOUT 10 CUPS

⅔ cup chopped onion

1 rib celery, finely chopped

¼ cup finely chopped red or orange bell pepper (optional)

2 tablespoons olive oil

4½ cups water

1 rounded tablespoon chicken bouillon powder or base

1½ cups diced ham

¼ teaspoon pepper

2 (15-ounce) cans corn, drained, or about 16 ounces frozen corn, thawed

4 tablespoons butter

4 tablespoons all-purpose flour

1 cup half-and-half

2 rounded tablespoons prepared Basil Pesto (see page 10)

In a medium soup pot over medium-high heat, briefly sauté the onion, celery, and bell pepper, in oil for about 2 minutes. Add the water, bouillon, and ham. Cover with a lid and simmer for about 5 to 7 minutes. Stir in the corn, and bring back to a simmer.

In a separate pan, melt the butter and stir in the flour to make a roux. Stir roux into the soup, stirring constantly while the soup thickens. Add the half-and-half and pesto. Bring to a low boil and taste. Adjust seasoning as needed.

TIP: It's nearly impossible to make a delicious soup by simply following the measurements in a recipe. Always taste your soup and adjust to your liking before serving. For this recipe, possible adjustments to texture and flavor can be made using half-and-half, bouillon, pepper, and/or pesto.

grilled salmon chowder

A delectable alternative to clam chowder! Pretty enough to start a fancy dinner with guests and tasty enough to please a picky palate.

MAKES 6 TO 8 SERVINGS

1 pound salmon fillet
½ teaspoon salt
1 teaspoon dill weed
Juice of 2 lemons, divided
3 tablespoons olive oil
2 tablespoons butter

1 small onion, diced
1 leek, cleaned and diced
1 clove garlic, minced
1 green bell pepper, diced
1 red bell pepper, diced
½ cup all-purpose flour

2 russet potatoes, peeled and finely diced
2 (14.5-ounce) cans chicken broth
1 cup whipping cream
1 cup milk

Grill the salmon just until you can flake it with a fork; it can be slightly underdone in the center, as it will continue to cook in the soup. Sprinkle the salt, dill, and 2 tablespoons lemon juice over the flesh side as it cooks. Transfer fish to a plate and remove the skin. Flake into small bite-size pieces. Set aside.

In a large saucepan, heat the oil and butter over medium heat; sauté the onion, leek, and garlic for about 5 minutes, stirring frequently. Add the bell peppers and sauté for 3 to 5 minutes more; stir in the flour. Add the potatoes and broth. Stir, and bring to a boil over medium-high heat. Reduce heat and simmer for about 12 minutes, or until potatoes are tender, stirring frequently to prevent sticking. Add the salmon, cream, milk, and remaining lemon juice. Let simmer for about 5 minutes, stirring frequently.

white clam chowder

Adding clams to the chowder just before the finish, after the boiling is done, helps prevent them from becoming rubbery. The hot soup will heat the clams without any boiling at all.

2 pounds russet potatoes, peeled and diced

5 ribs celery, finely diced

$\frac{1}{2}$ small onion, finely diced (about $\frac{1}{2}$ cup)

1 large leek, diced (white part plus about 3 inches of green)

2 tablespoons red wine vinegar

$\frac{1}{2}$ cup diced bell pepper (any color)

2 bay leaves

$\frac{1}{2}$ teaspoon dried thyme leaves

2 teaspoons salt, plus more

$\frac{1}{2}$ teaspoon pepper, plus more

Water to cover

1 stick (8 tablespoons) butter

10 tablespoons all-purpose flour

3 cups half-and-half, divided

3 shakes ($\frac{1}{4}$ teaspoon) hot sauce, plus more

2–3 (6-ounce) cans chopped clams, with juice

Place the potatoes, celery, onion, leek, vinegar, bell pepper, bay leaves, thyme, salt, and pepper in a large soup pot and cover with water. Cover pot with a lid and bring to a boil. Reduce heat to a low boil and cook until vegetables are tender, about 30 minutes.

Meanwhile, make a roux by cooking the butter and flour together in a skillet for 4 to 5 minutes. Stir frequently to avoid burning. Thin the roux with hot soup liquid until it has the texture of thick paste.

When vegetables are cooked but still simmering, add the roux and whisk to incorporate well while soup thickens. Add the half-and-half and hot sauce, and then bring to a low boil. Turn off heat and stir in the clams. Let sit for 5 minutes while the clams heat through. Taste and adjust seasonings with salt, pepper, and additional hot sauce.

garlicky potato dumpling stew

The garlicky flavor in this stew comes from the pesto. I make my own (recipe page 10), but if you have a favorite store brand, feel free to substitute.

————— MAKES 6 SERVINGS —————

1 (16-ounce) package potato gnocchi

1 (14.5-ounce) can vegetable broth

2 cups water

1 tablespoon vegetable bouillon powder

1 tablespoon plus 1 teaspoon Knorr chicken bouillon powder or Better Than Bouillon chicken base

3–4 tablespoons Basil Pesto (page 10)

2 cups half-and-half

2 tablespoons cornstarch dissolved in 4 tablespoons water

$\frac{1}{2}$ teaspoon salt

$\frac{1}{8}$ teaspoon pepper

Grated Parmesan cheese, for garnish

In a large saucepan, cook gnocchi according to package directions. When dumplings float to the top, they're done. Drain water and transfer gnocchi to a bowl while you make the soup.

In the same saucepan, combine the broth, water, vegetable bouillon, chicken bullion, pesto, half-and-half, cornstarch mixture, salt, and pepper. Bring to a boil over high heat, stirring constantly, and then reduce to low. Return gnocchi back to the pan and let soup simmer for 1 to 2 minutes while dumplings reheat. Serve with a sprinkling of cheese for garnish.

meat, poultry & fish bowls

beef with barley stew

In lieu of cooking on the stove, this recipe can be halved and made in a slow cooker (high for 4 to 6 hours or low for 6 to 8 hours). For slow cooking, I recommend the tomatoey variation.

2 pounds stew meat or cubed rump roast

2 tablespoons oil

1 (14.5-ounce) can diced or crushed tomatoes, with juice

3 (14.5-ounce) cans beef broth

4 cups water, divided

1 cup pearl barley

2 tablespoons dehydrated onion flakes

1 bay leaf

2 teaspoons dried thyme leaves

2 carrots, peeled and diced

2 (14.5-ounce) cans green beans, drained

1 (14.5-ounce) can corn, drained (optional)

2 teaspoons soy sauce

½ teaspoon pepper

Salt

Beef bouillon (optional)

In a large soup pot, working in batches, brown the meat evenly in oil over medium-high heat; do not overcrowd the pan. Deglaze the bottom of the pot with the tomatoes. Add broth and return meat to the pot. Simmer for 1½ to 2 hours, until meat is tender.

Add 2 cups water to the pot, the barley, onion, bay leaf, and thyme. Bring to a boil, reduce to simmer, and cook for about 40 minutes, until the barley is tender. Add the carrots, green beans, corn, soy sauce, pepper, and salt to taste, and remaining 2 cups water or more if needed; bring to a boil. Reduce to a steady simmer and cook for 15 minutes, until carrots are tender. Taste and adjust seasonings, adding a little beef bouillon if desired.

VARIATIONS: For a slightly sweeter Beef and Cabbage Stew, add 1 to 2 cups shredded cabbage when adding the barley.

For Tomatoey Beef-Barley Stew, add 2 tablespoons tomato paste plus ½ cup ketchup along with the water.

vegetable beef stew in gravy

This stew takes a little while to make, but it's well worth the effort. For a switch-up, try adding cooked home-style noodles in place of the potatoes. And for real decadence, top each serving with a dollop of sour cream.

2 tablespoons olive oil

1 1/2–2 pounds round steak, cut into 1/2-inch cubes

2 onions, sliced

2 cloves garlic, minced

Juice of 1 lemon

3–4 quarts water, divided

3 ribs celery, sliced

6 carrots, sliced

1–2 parsnips, peeled, halved lengthwise, and sliced

4 potatoes, peeled, quartered, and sliced

4 ounces sliced mushrooms (optional)

2 bay leaves

1 teaspoon paprika

1/2 teaspoon allspice

2 teaspoons Worcestershire sauce

1/2 cup all-purpose flour mixed into 3/4 cup water

3 teaspoons beef bouillon powder or base

Salt and pepper

2 tablespoons chopped fresh parsley

In a large soup pot, heat the oil over medium-high heat and brown the meat. Remove meat from pot and set aside. Brown onions and garlic in the meat drippings for 2 to 3 minutes. Add lemon juice to the pot and deglaze. Return meat to pot and add 1 quart of water. Cover and bring to a boil; reduce heat and let meat simmer with onion and garlic for about 2 hours while the meat tenderizes. Add the celery, carrots, parsnips, potatoes, mushrooms, bay leaves, paprika, allspice, Worcestershire, and enough of the remaining water to cover vegetables by 1 inch. Cover pot and bring to a boil; reduce heat to a low boil and let cook for 30 to 35 minutes.

Whisk the flour and water mixture together and stir into the bubbling stew. Stir constantly for about 3 minutes while the liquid thickens. Season with bouillon to taste, starting with 2 teaspoons and adding more if desired. Adjust seasoning to taste with salt and pepper. Finish the stew by stirring in fresh parsley.

taco soup

Yum, yum! Kids and adults alike love the comfort that taco soup delivers.

1 tablespoon olive oil

1 pound ground beef or turkey

1 onion, chopped

1 (28-ounce) can crushed tomatoes

2 (15-ounce) cans tomato sauce

3 cups water

2 (15.5-ounce) cans kidney beans, drained

16 ounces corn, frozen, thawed, or canned, drained

1 (6-ounce) can sliced black olives, drained

1 (1.25-ounce) packet taco seasoning

1/4 teaspoon garlic powder

Salt

Toppings: grated cheddar or Jack cheese, sour cream, corn chips, sliced green onion, diced avocado or guacamole

In a skillet, heat the olive oil and brown the meat and onion together until meat is cooked (divide into 2 batches so as not to crowd the pan). Drain grease and transfer meat-onion mixture to a soup pot. Add remaining ingredients except the toppings. Bring soup to a boil then reduce to a simmer; cook, covered, for about 20 to 30 minutes, allowing flavors to meld. Ladle into bowls and top as desired.

mom's beef stew

Everybody has a few favorite dishes their mom made, and this is one of mine. Mom would make stew on cold winter days, and it would be ready for supper when we got home from school. The recipe is very basic; the long cooking develops a flavorful broth while the potatoes thicken it a bit (especially when reheated the next day). I always stirred a little ketchup into mine at the table.

―――――――― MAKES ABOUT 4 QUARTS ――――――――

1 ½ pounds cubed beef
  stew meat
2 tablespoons vegetable oil
2 onions, sliced
3 quarts water, divided

5 ribs celery, sliced
8–10 carrots, sliced
3–4 large baking potatoes,
  peeled, quartered, and
  sliced

Salt and pepper
Ketchup (optional)
Fresh thyme leaves, for
  garnish

In a large soup pot, brown the beef in hot oil. Add the onion and brown for 2 to 3 minutes longer. Pour in 1 quart water and stir to remove brown bits from the bottom of the pan. Cover pot and bring to a boil; reduce heat and let simmer for 1 ½ to 2 hours.

Add the vegetables and 2 quarts water to the pot. Cover, bring to a boil, and then reduce heat and let simmer for 1 more hour, until beef is tender. Season with salt and pepper to taste. Pass ketchup at the table as an optional stir-in condiment, and garnish with thyme.

curry turkey and rice soup

Precook the rice and use some leftover turkey to make this soup in a snap. It can easily be doubled.

2 (14.5-ounce) cans chicken broth

$\frac{1}{3}$ cup water

2 tablespoons butter

2 tablespoons plus 1 teaspoon all-purpose flour

1 tablespoon dehydrated chopped onion

2 teaspoons chicken bouillon powder or 2 small cubes chicken bouillon

$\frac{1}{2}$ teaspoon ground sage

$\frac{1}{2}$ teaspoon dried thyme leaves

1 teaspoon curry powder

1 heaping cup cooked rice

1 $\frac{1}{2}$ cups diced cooked turkey

1 $\frac{1}{2}$ cups frozen mixed vegetables, thawed

1 cup milk

Salt and pepper

Heat the broth and water to boiling in a large saucepan; reduce heat to simmer.

Meanwhile, cook the butter and flour together in a small frying pan for 3 to 4 minutes to make a roux. Thin the roux with small additions of hot broth, stirring each thoroughly into the roux before adding more. After adding about 1 cup of liquid, whisk the roux back into the remaining hot broth until it is well blended and starts to thicken. Increase heat to medium high and add the remaining ingredients, except salt and pepper. Stir well and let soup simmer for about 10 minutes while flavors meld and liquid thickens. Season to taste with salt and pepper.

asian pork noodle bowls

Succulent, thin slices of pork join bamboo shoots and rice noodles in a rich broth. I recommend using chopsticks to slurp up the noodles and veggies and then lifting the bowl up to your mouth with both hands to drink all the goodness that remains.

─────── MAKES 4 SERVINGS ───────

2 (14.5-ounce) cans chicken broth

4 teaspoons soy sauce or tamari

12 tablespoons chopped green onion tops

½ pound pork loin,* thinly sliced lengthwise

Seasoned salt

2 tablespoons oil

1 (8-ounce) can bamboo shoots, drained

½ pound sliced mushrooms

2 teaspoons butter

2 teaspoons peanut oil or other cooking oil**

2 tablespoons water

8 leaves Chinese cabbage (napa or savoy)

6–8 ounces maifun rice noodles

In a medium-size pot over medium heat, bring the broth, soy sauce, and green onions to a simmer.

Meanwhile, rub each long slice of pork loin lightly on both sides with seasoned salt then cut into bite-size lengths. In a frying pan over medium-high heat, lightly brown the meat on both sides in 2 tablespoons oil. Work in small batches; do not crowd the pan. Transfer cooked meat to the simmering broth, and add the bamboo shoots. (Reserve the frying pan for cooking mushrooms.)

*Freezing the loin for 30 to 45 minutes ahead of time makes it easier to slice thinly.

**If you like the flavor of sesame oil, you could substitute it for 1 teaspoon of the peanut oil.

>> continued on 79

In the frying pan, braise the mushrooms over low heat in the butter, peanut oil, and 2 tablespoons water. Cook for 4 to 5 minutes, stirring frequently. Add mushrooms and all their liquid to the soup pot.

Wash the cabbage leaves and cut away and discard the thickest part of the tough stems. Cut leaves into large bite-size pieces and add to the pot. Place a lid on the pot and simmer the soup while you prepare the noodles.

Cook the noodles according to package directions. Divide the cooked noodles among four bowls. Distribute the meat and vegetables among the bowls and then pour the broth over the noodles. Shlurp!

sweet ham and vegetable soup

Balancing the sugar and salt in this soup requires tasting; add salt as the last step, about ½ teaspoon at a time until your palate says "Perfection."

2–3 tablespoons olive oil

1 large onion, chopped

4 ribs celery, chopped

6 carrots, peeled and chopped

2 pounds red potatoes, peeled and diced

3 cups diced cooked ham

1 bay leaf

1 ½ teaspoons dried oregano

1 teaspoon seasoned salt

6 cups water

3 (14.5-ounce) cans chicken broth

1 (15-ounce) can green beans, drained

1 (15-ounce) can red kidney beans, drained and rinsed

1 (15-ounce) can great Northern beans, drained and rinsed

1 quart or 2 (15-ounce) cans crushed or diced tomatoes

1 (6-ounce) can tomato paste

2 tablespoons brown sugar, or ½ cup drippings from glazed ham

2 teaspoons Worcestershire sauce

Salt and pepper

In a large soup pot, heat oil over medium-high heat. Sauté the onion, celery, and carrots together for about 8 minutes while onion turns translucent and vegetables begin to cook. Add the potatoes, ham, bay leaf, oregano, seasoned salt, water, and broth. Cover pot and bring to a boil over medium high, stirring occasionally; reduce heat and let simmer for about 30 minutes, until vegetables are tender.

Add all the beans, tomatoes, tomato paste, brown sugar, and Worcestershire sauce. Bring to a boil again; reduce heat and simmer for 15 minutes while flavors meld. Adjust seasoning with salt and pepper.

country sausage and rice soup

This is a uniquely satisfying soup. For a twofer, divide the soup in half once the rice is cooked. Proceed with the recipe for the first half, and add the variation ingredients to the second half.

2 tablespoons oil

1 pound country sausage

4 cups hot water

4 ounces chopped fresh mushrooms or 1 (4-ounce) can mushroom pieces, drained

1 rib celery, finely chopped

1 tablespoon dehydrated chopped onion

1 (2-ounce) jar chopped pimentos, drained

2 teaspoons chicken bouillon powder or base, plus more as needed

¾ cup wild rice blend

1 cup half-and-half

1 (5-ounce) jar Kraft pimento spread*

Heat the oil in a medium pot and brown the sausage, crumbling it while it cooks.

Add the water and bring to a boil while adding the mushrooms, celery, onion, pimentos, bouillon, and rice. Stir, cover with a lid, and reduce to a simmer until rice is tender, about 15 minutes. Add more water as needed to maintain the soup's liquid. Taste and adjust with ½ teaspoon bouillon at a time, if needed.

Stir in half-and-half and cheese. Let simmer for a few minutes for flavors to meld.

*Alternatively, use 1 cup grated cheddar cheese.

VARIATION: For Sausage, Limas, and Tomato Soup, divide the soup in half after the rice is cooked. To the second half, add 1 (8-ounce) can chopped tomatoes, ½ cup frozen lima beans, ⅛ teaspoon garlic powder, and a dash of hot sauce (optional). Cover and simmer until the beans have softened.

turkey vegetable stew
with dumplings

A warming meal for a chilly day, this stew has an aroma that will bring the troops in a hurry.

STEW

3 tablespoons olive oil

1 pound ground turkey

1 small onion, diced

3 russet potatoes, diced

5 carrots, sliced

4 cups chicken broth

2 cups water

2 teaspoons salt

$\frac{1}{2}$ teaspoon pepper

2 teaspoons poultry
seasoning

1 teaspoon dried marjoram

1 pound frozen peas,
thawed, or 1 (15-ounce)
can peas, drained

2 envelopes turkey or
chicken gravy mix

DUMPLINGS*

1 cup all-purpose flour

$1\frac{1}{2}$ teaspoons baking
powder

$\frac{1}{4}$ teaspoon salt

2 teaspoons dried parsley

2 tablespoons butter, room
temperature

$\frac{1}{2}$ cup milk, plus more as
needed

STEW

In a large saucepan, heat the oil and brown the turkey and onion together, stirring and crumbling turkey. Add the potatoes, carrots, broth, water, salt, pepper, poultry seasoning, and marjoram. Cover and bring to a boil over medium-high heat. Reduce heat to a low boil and let cook until potatoes are tender.

DUMPLINGS

In a medium mixing bowl combine the flour, baking powder, salt, and parsley. Cut in the butter using a pastry cutter or by pinching it with your fingers until you have crumbles the size of peas.

Add the milk and stir with a fork just to combine. If dough seems dry and crumbly, add more milk, 2 tablespoons at a time, until it is the consistency of a brownie batter.

TO FINISH

Add the peas and the contents of the gravy packets to the soup and stir. Divide the dough into 8 spoonfuls and drop onto the surface of the stew. Bring to a simmer. Cover pan and let biscuits steam until cooked through, 10 to 12 minutes. Serve 1 dumpling per bowl and ladle stew over.

*Alternatively, use a can of refrigerator biscuits for the dumplings. These will cook in 8 to 10 minutes.

country-style chicken noodle soup

Two things most chicken noodle soup recipes have in common are . . . chicken and noodles—and even those can differ from recipe to recipe. Home-style noodles push the satisfaction quotient over the top!

——— MAKES 4 TO 6 SERVINGS ———

2 (14.5-ounce) cans chicken broth

3 cups water

2 teaspoons chicken bouillon powder or base

1 small onion, chopped

3 carrots, sliced

4 ribs celery, sliced

1 bay leaf

1 (14.5-ounce) can corn, drained

2½ cups chopped roasted chicken

2 teaspoons salt

¼ teaspoon freshly ground black pepper

8 ounces wide egg noodles

Bring the broth and water to a boil in a large saucepan. Add the bouillon, onion, carrots, celery, and bay leaf. Cover the pan and boil on medium heat until vegetables are tender, about 15 minutes.

Stir in the corn, chicken, salt, and pepper; return to boiling for 2 minutes. Add noodles to the soup; cook at a medium boil until noodles are al dente, about 7 minutes. Remove pan from heat and keep covered until ready to serve. Noodles will continue to soften in the hot broth.

simple chicken and dumplings

Chicken and dumplings has all the makings of comfort plus! Nothing else satisfies the taste buds and warms the soul better. Convenience ingredients make this a fast and easy weeknight meal.

2 (14.5-ounce) cans chicken broth

2 cups grated carrot

2 (14.5-ounce) cans condensed cream of chicken soup

2 cups shredded or cubed precooked chicken, or 1 (12.5-ounce) can chicken, drained

1 (16.3 ounce) can large (grand) refrigerator biscuits*

Pepper

Chopped fresh parsley, for garnish

Pour broth into a large soup pot and heat to boiling. Add carrots and bring back to a boil. Whisk in cream of chicken soup, add chicken, and bring to a boil. Set all 8 biscuits in the broth (squeeze them together if your pan isn't wide enough for a comfortable fit), cover with a lid, and reduce heat to medium low. Steam the biscuits in simmering soup for 8 to 10 minutes without removing the lid.

To serve, lift biscuits from pot into serving bowls, and then ladle soup over the biscuits. Sprinkle with pepper and parsley.

*Alternatively, make your own dumplings. See recipe on page 82.

chicken rack soup

Making broth by boiling bones was a thrifty practice in our great-great-grandmothers' day, but then it disappeared for a few generations and was substituted with convenience. Now people are again appreciating the health benefits and dollar savings of making bone broth. Save bones and skin from your rotisserie chickens, or those you cook yourself, in the freezer until you have enough to extract their goodness through long cooking for a soup.

MAKES 4 SERVINGS

2–3 chicken racks and skin
6 cups water
1 small onion
3 carrots, peeled and sliced
2 potatoes, peeled and cubed

3 ribs celery, sliced
1 bay leaf
1 teaspoon salt
½ teaspoon pepper
1 (14.5-ounce) can chicken broth (optional)

1 teaspoon (or more) chicken bouillon powder or base
1–2 cups shredded or diced precooked chicken

Place the chicken bones in a 5-quart or larger slow cooker and nearly cover with water. Cook on high for about 2 hours; the liquid should be boiling. Turn to low and let simmer for 2 to 2½ hours. Turn off cooker. Remove and discard solids with a slotted spoon. Refrigerate the stock overnight in the crock.

The next day, lift the solid grease from the broth and discard it. The stock will likely be a solid gel. Let crock warm to room temperature; then turn slow cooker to high until gel is liquefied. Meanwhile, add all vegetables and seasonings. The vegetables should be covered with liquid. If more liquid is needed to cover, add 1 can chicken broth or your favorite bouillon plus water. Cook for 3 to 4 hours on low. Add chicken during last 1 to 2 hours of cooking. Taste soup and adjust flavor with bouillon, adding just a little at a time and tasting after each addition.

chicken enchilada soup

The hardest thing about making this soup is poaching the chicken breasts. I cook mine in a covered casserole in a 350-degree oven for about 50 minutes then turn off the heat and leave the chicken in the oven for about another hour. It comes out perfectly tender.

2–3 chicken breasts, poached in 1 $^1/_2$ cups water, liquid reserved

4 cups water, divided

2 tablespoons Better Than Bouillon chicken base

1 cup long-grain rice

1 $^1/_2$ teaspoons cumin

1 (15-ounce) can green enchilada sauce (medium heat)

1 (15-ounce) can white beans (great Northern or cannellini), drained

1 (15-ounce) can corn, drained, or frozen kernels, thawed (optional)

Garnishes: sour cream, grated cheese, blue corn tortilla chips, avocado, chopped fresh tomatoes, cilantro, squeeze of lime

After poaching the chicken breasts, let the meat cool enough to handle. Reserve the poaching liquid for the soup. Shred and break meat into bite-size pieces.

In a medium pot, bring 2 cups water to a boil and add the bouillon and rice. Stir and cover. Reduce to a simmer and cook until the water has been absorbed, stirring once to be sure it isn't sticking, about 20 minutes.

Pour the reserved poaching liquid into the rice. Add the cumin, remaining 2 cups water, enchilada sauce, beans, and corn. Stir together and heat. Taste and adjust flavor to your liking with another teaspoon of bouillon.

Divide among bowls and garnish as desired.

chicken with gnocchi soup

This is the epitome of comfort foods, in my book. I enjoy it so much at Olive Garden that I made my own version, and everyone who has tasted it swoons over the creamy, rich flavor. Gnocchi can be found in the pasta section of the supermarket.

MAKES 10 SERVINGS

2 tablespoons olive oil
1 tablespoon butter
3 ribs celery, diced small
2 cloves garlic, minced
2 large carrots, grated
⅓ cup all-purpose flour
2½ cups diced cooked chicken

2 quarts chicken broth
2 cups half-and-half
1 cup whipping cream
1½ tablespoons cornstarch mixed with 2 tablespoons water
1 pound potato gnocchi with Parmesan, or plain

6 ounces fresh spinach, chopped
2 teaspoons chicken bouillon powder or base (optional)
Freshly ground black pepper

In a medium saucepan, heat olive oil and butter over medium heat. Sauté celery and garlic for about 3 minutes then add carrots and continue sautéing for about 2 minutes more. Add flour and toss with vegetables to distribute. Continue cooking for about 4 minutes, stirring occasionally, while vegetables soften and flour cooks.

Add chicken and broth; bring to a boil. Add half-and-half and cream and return to a boil. Thicken broth with cornstarch mixture, stirring rapidly to avoid lumps. Reduce heat to low.

Cook gnocchi according to package directions. As gnocchi float to the top, transfer them with a slotted spoon to the soup. Increase heat to medium high, stirring, until soup begins to bubble. Stir in spinach. Cook for about 1 minute then taste. Season with bouillon and pepper to taste.

red whitefish stew

There are many different kinds of tummy-warming fisherman's stew. I am not a fisherman, so I get mine at the market and choose fish with firm flesh.

2 tablespoons olive oil
1 medium onion, chopped
3 ribs celery, thinly sliced
½ cup chopped green bell pepper
3 carrots, diced
1 (14.5-ounce) can chicken broth
1 (8-ounce) jar clam juice

3 cups water, divided
1–1½ pounds firm-fleshed whitefish (cod, halibut, tilapia, swordfish, etc.), thawed if previously frozen
1 (12-ounce) jar roasted red peppers, drained and chopped

2 (14.5-ounce) cans stewed or diced tomatoes
1½ teaspoons Cajun seasoning
Salt and pepper
5–6 cups cooked white rice, hot
¼ cup chopped fresh parsley, for garnish

In a large saucepan, heat the oil over medium heat and sauté the onion, celery, and bell pepper until the onion turns translucent. Add carrots, broth, clam juice, and enough water to just cover. Cover pan and bring to a boil; reduce heat to avoid boilovers. Cook until vegetables are soft, 20 to 25 minutes.

Meanwhile, cut the fish into pieces about ¾ inch square. Set aside.

Add the peppers, tomatoes, and seasoning to the vegetables and bring to a low boil. Add the fish to the soup and press with a spoon to submerge. Cover pan and simmer for 15 to 20 minutes, until fish is cooked. Season with salt and pepper to taste.

To serve, place a mound of rice in each bowl and ladle the soup around it. Garnish with parsley.

lemon chicken soup

One of my favorite things to order at a Greek restaurant is tender chicken kebabs with lemon rice. This soup draws on those flavors and is extra delicious served with warm pita bread.

MAKES 8 TO 10 SERVINGS

GREEK RICE PILAF

3 tablespoons olive oil

3 tablespoons butter

1 cup finely chopped onion

2 cups uncooked long-grain white rice

4 cups chicken broth

½ cup lemon juice

1 ½ teaspoons dried oregano

2 teaspoons salt

SOUP

3 boneless, skinless chicken breasts, trimmed

6 cups water

Better Than Bouillon chicken base or chicken bouillon powder

Salt

Freshly ground black pepper

Lemon zest (optional)

PILAF

In a medium saucepan, heat the oil and butter over medium heat and sauté the onion for 5 to 7 minutes, stirring, until onion turns translucent. Add the rice, broth, lemon juice, oregano, and salt. Cover pan, bring to a boil, and then reduce heat and simmer for 30 minutes, or until rice is soft to the bite. Stir occasionally so rice doesn't stick. Reserve 2 to 3 cups cooked rice for the soup.

SOUP

Slice the chicken breasts lengthwise about ½ inch thick and then dice. Place the chicken and water in a large saucepan and bring quickly to a boil. Reduce to a low boil and let cook for 30 to 40 minutes, until chicken is tender. Skim fat solids from the broth. Add reserved rice to the soup and more water if desired. Taste and adjust seasonings with bouillon, salt, and pepper. Garnish each bowl of soup with zest if desired.

luscious legumes

ham bone soup

One of the best things about a bone-in ham is being able to make this hearty soup using the bone and the meat that clings onto it after all the sandwiches have been made.

———— MAKES 10 SERVINGS ————

1 pound dried white beans, soaked and prepared for cooking
1 ham bone with meat
1 large onion, chopped
5 ribs celery, chopped

6–8 carrots, chopped
1 bay leaf
8–10 cups water
1–2 cups chopped ham

2 tablespoons chicken bouillon powder or base (or ham base if available)
1 tablespoon prepared honey mustard
$\frac{1}{2}$ teaspoon pepper
Salt (optional)

Drain the beans. Place all ingredients except salt in a large soup pot. Cover and bring to a boil, and then reduce heat and simmer soup for $2\frac{1}{2}$ to 4 hours, until beans are softened to your liking. Alternatively, cook in a large slow cooker on low heat for 8 to 10 hours.

Remove ham bone from the soup, and when cool enough to handle, pick off any bits of ham to return to the soup (be careful not to add gristle or too much fat). Taste the soup and adjust seasoning with salt if needed.

lima bean soup

I was an unusual kid: I really *liked* the lima bean soup the cafeteria cooks served for school lunch. My recipe isn't exactly like theirs, but the mild flavor isn't overburdened with salt, which is a plus. You'll need to soak your dried beans overnight.

——————— MAKES 10 TO 12 SERVINGS ———————

1 (16-ounce) bag dried baby lima beans

6 cups cold water, for soaking

1 large onion, diced

3 ribs celery, finely diced

5 carrots, peeled and finely diced

2 (14.5-ounce) cans chicken broth

3 cups finely diced ham

Water

Salt and pepper

3–4 slices bacon, finely chopped and cooked crisp, for garnish

Soak the beans in cool water for at least 8 hours or overnight. Drain and discard water.

Place the beans, onion, celery, carrots, broth, and ham in a 5- to 6-quart slow cooker. Add enough water to cover. Cook for 6 to 8 hours on low, until the beans are cooked to your liking. Taste the broth and adjust flavor with salt and pepper. Garnish with crumbled bacon.

bean with bacon soup

This is remarkably like the commercial variety in the red and white can. If you want to start with dry beans, you might need to increase salt to taste at the end of cooking.

2 (15-ounce) cans great Northern beans, drained and rinsed

2 cups water

4 tablespoons tomato sauce

3 tablespoons crispy crumbled bacon

2 teaspoons bacon grease

1 carrot, finely grated

1 teaspoon cornstarch

1 teaspoon salt

1 teaspoon sugar

½ teaspoon onion powder

½ teaspoon liquid smoke

Place all ingredients in a medium saucepan and bring to a low boil, stirring frequently. When hot, remove from heat and let cool a little. Remove 1 to 1 ½ cups soup and set aside. Using a hand-held blender, purée the soup to a smooth consistency. If you use a stand blender, add a bit more water if needed for the blender to operate. Return reserved soup to the saucepan, stir well, and heat through.

sweet-pepper chicken soup

In September, the peppers in my garden morph from green to red and a variety of colors in between. That is when I enjoy making this soup. At other times of the year, I use mini sweet peppers from the market. This soup develops better flavor if refrigerated overnight and served the next day.

1 small onion, quartered and thickly sliced

2 ribs celery, sliced

1–1¼ cups diced sweet bell peppers (any colors)

2 tablespoons vegetable oil

2 large carrots, peeled and diced

3 cups chicken broth

2 (15-ounce) cans great Northern or other white beans, drained and rinsed

1 (4-ounce) can diced green chiles

2 cups diced cooked chicken

½ teaspoon seasoned salt

¼ teaspoon garlic powder

1 teaspoon salt

½ teaspoon hot sauce, plus more to taste

2 teaspoons lime juice

1 bay leaf

½ teaspoon dried cilantro, or 1 small handful fresh cilantro, chopped

In a soup pot, sauté the onion, celery, and bell pepper in oil for about 5 minutes, until partly tender. Add the carrots and cook for 2 minutes more. Add the broth, beans, chiles, chicken, seasoned salt, garlic powder, salt, hot sauce, lime juice, bay leaf, and cilantro plus enough water to cover. Cover with a lid and bring to a boil. Cook on medium high for 3 to 5 minutes, and then reduce to a simmer for about 20 minutes to blend flavors. Taste a spoonful (not just the liquid on the tip of a spoon, or you won't get the full flavor) for flavor base, heat, and saltiness. Adjust as desired.

vegetarian chili

At least once each winter, I get a tremendous craving for bean chili. I tell myself it's because my body wants protein, but really, I think it's a throwback to childhood, when my mom made the best chili I ever tasted.

MAKES 8 TO 10 SERVINGS

4 tablespoons olive oil
1 onion, chopped
2 cloves garlic, minced
1 cup chopped carrot
¾ cup chopped celery
½ cup chopped green or
 red bell pepper

4 (14.5-ounce) cans beans
 (1 can each kidney, black,
 pinto, red), drained and
 rinsed
2 (10-ounce) cans diced
 tomatoes with chiles
2 (14.5-ounce) cans diced
 tomatoes
2 (14.5-ounce) cans corn,
 drained
2 teaspoons cumin

1 teaspoon chili powder
1 ½ teaspoons dried
 epazote* (optional)
1 teaspoon Mexican
 oregano
2 teaspoons salt
1 teaspoon liquid smoke
Garnishes: sour cream,
 grated cheese, sliced
 green onions, and/or
 corn chips

In a large soup pot, heat oil over medium-high heat until it shimmers. Add the onion, garlic, carrot, and celery to the pot and stir to coat with oil. Sauté for 8 to 10 minutes, stirring frequently.

Add all the remaining ingredients (except garnish). Cover the pot and bring to a boil; reduce heat and simmer for 30 to 45 minutes, stirring occasionally. If the soup gets too dry, add 1 cup water to prevent sticking. Serve with garnishes as desired.

*Epazote is a Mexican herb that will help reduce flatulence from the beans but also add its own flavor. If you cannot find this ingredient, double the amount of Mexican oregano, which is somewhat different in flavor from Italian oregano.

pork and beans soup

If you want to get a twofer, roast a loin of pork for a meal and use a portion of it for this soup. I like the flavor that a crusty brown exterior gives to the loin; you may prefer it without. The juices and brown bits from cooking the pork make a great start for the soup.

————— MAKES ABOUT 3 QUARTS —————

1 small onion, chopped
2 cloves garlic, chopped
1 tablespoon oil
1½ teaspoons cumin
2½ cups diced roast pork loin

Juices from the deglazed roasting pan, plus enough water to make 4 cups
1 (14.5-ounce) can diced tomatoes, plus 1 can water
1 (14.5-ounce) can black beans, drained and rinsed

1 (14.5-ounce) can white beans, drained and rinsed
2 teaspoons chili powder
1 Knorr beef bouillon cube, plus more as needed
Pepper
Salt (optional)

In a 4-quart saucepan or larger, sauté the onion and garlic in oil over medium heat for about 3 minutes. Add cumin and continue sautéing for 2 more minutes.

Add the pork juices plus water, tomatoes plus water, pork, beans, chili powder, and bouillon. Bring to a boil over medium-high heat and then reduce to a steady low boil. Cook for about 30 minutes while flavors meld. Add more water if needed.

Taste and adjust flavor and seasonings with additional bouillon, pepper, and salt.

VARIATION: For Pork and Beans with Veggies, try any or all of these robust additions: corn, celery, carrots, shredded cabbage, and cubed orange winter squash. You will need to increase the water to cover the solid ingredients in the pan by at least 1 inch. Taste and adjust the flavor base with more beef bouillon, adding just 1 to 2 teaspoons at a time.

lentils, chick peas, and greens

As written, this recipe is vegetarian. But either beef or chicken broth can be substituted for the vegetable broth. Heart-healthy lentils have good amounts of fiber and help lower cholesterol.

MAKES 4 SERVINGS

2 tablespoons olive oil

2 carrots, chopped

1 onion, chopped

1–2 cloves garlic, minced

2 ribs celery, chopped

4 cups water

1 (14.5-ounce) can vegetable broth

1 (15-ounce) can chick peas, drained and rinsed

1 Knorr vegetable bouillon cube

¼ teaspoon chili powder

¼ teaspoon cumin

1 teaspoon Worcestershire sauce

1 cup brown or green lentils, picked over and rinsed

4 cups chopped fresh cooking greens (e.g., spinach, kale, and/or chard)

Salt and pepper

In a large saucepan, heat the olive oil and sauté the carrots, onion, garlic, and celery for 4 to 5 minutes, until the onion begins to turn translucent. Add the water, broth, chick peas, bouillon, chili powder, cumin, Worcestershire sauce, and lentils. Cover and bring to a boil then reduce to a steady simmer; cook for about 30 minutes, or until vegetables and lentils are tender. Add the greens and cook, covered, for another 4 to 5 minutes. Season to taste with salt and pepper.

mediterranean red lentil stew

In the book of Genesis, the famished Esau traded his birthright to his brother Jacob for a bowl of red lentil stew. While I don't think it was worth *that* much, a cupful of red lentil stew is a fine antidote for tummy-rumbling hunger.

MAKES 8 TO 10 SERVINGS

2 tablespoons olive oil
1 medium onion, diced
4 ribs celery, thinly sliced
5–6 carrots, diced
1 medium sweet potato, diced ½ small head cabbage, thinly sliced
1½ cups dried red lentils

1/4 cup pearl barley
1/2 cup golden raisins
4 cups vegetable broth
4 cups water
4 cubes Knorr vegetable bouillon
1–2 tablespoons tomato paste (optional)

2 teaspoons dried oregano leaves
1½ teaspoons curry powder
½ teaspoon dried thyme leaves
½ teaspoon ground cloves
½ teaspoon garlic powder
Salt and pepper

In a large saucepan, heat oil over medium-high heat. Sauté the onion, celery, and carrots, stirring frequently, until onion turns translucent. Add remaining ingredients except salt and pepper; bring to a boil. Reduce heat to a steady simmer, cover pan, and cook for 25 minutes, until lentils are starting to become tender, stir frequently to avoid sticking. Add the cabbage and cook for 15 to 20 minutes more. Adjust seasonings with salt and pepper to taste.

VARIATIONS: For South of the Border Lentil Stew, use butternut squash instead of sweet potato. Omit the raisins. Then substitute cumin for the curry powder, add 2 tablespoons of canned diced green chiles, and squeeze in the juice of ½ lime.

best split pea soup

The trick with this soup is to find the sweet spot between the flavor of peas and the foundation flavor of meat underneath; making additions of your favorite chicken bouillon in small amounts, then tasting, is the most trusted way to achieve balance. Taste and adjust, taste and adjust.

MAKES 8 TO 10 SERVINGS

1 pound dried split peas
1 onion, chopped
6 cups water
1 bay leaf*

3 potatoes, cut into small dice
2 cups chopped carrots
2 ribs celery, chopped

3 cups diced cooked ham
1 tablespoon chicken bouillon or ham base
¼ teaspoon pepper

In a large saucepan, cover the peas and onion with water. Add the bay leaf, cover with a lid, and bring to a boil. (TIP: Dried peas foam up and boil over easily. Spraying a little oil over the peas beforehand prevents foaming, but if you forget, spraying oil onto the foam will make it subside.) Reduce heat to a low boil and cook until peas are tender, about 1½ hours.

Remove bay leaf and smash the peas with a potato masher. (If you prefer a smoother soup, remove and reserve about 2 cups of the peas, and purée those remaining in the pan. Return the reserved peas for texture.) In a separate large saucepan, cook the potatoes, carrots, celery, ham, bouillon, and pepper in enough water to just cover, until vegetables are tender.

Add the vegetables and meat to the peas, with as much of the vegetable cooking liquid as you like to thin the soup, and mix well. Simmer for about 30 minutes to meld flavors.

*A sprig of fresh rosemary can be substituted.

grilled chicken chili

I've been at chili cook-offs where the chicken chili has beat out all the beef-and-bean varieties. This recipe is a surefire family favorite. If your family can stand more heat, turn it up with jalapeños in place of diced green chiles. (TIP: Whenever you grill chicken, grill a few more pieces than you will need; slice and freeze it for later use.)

MAKES ABOUT 2 1/2 QUARTS

1 tablespoon olive oil
1 onion, diced
1–2 cloves garlic, minced
2 teaspoons cumin
1 1/2 teaspoons ground red chili powder
1 1/2 teaspoons Mexican oregano

1 (4-ounce) can diced green chiles
2 1/2 cups chicken broth
3 cups diced grilled chicken
1 (15-ounce) can corn, drained
2 (15.5-ounce) cans cannellini beans, drained

4 ounces cream cheese
15 ounces Mexican crema
Salt
Optional garnishes: cilantro, tortilla chips, sliced jalapeños; crumbled Mexican cheese

In a soup pot, heat the olive oil over medium heat and sauté the onion and garlic for 3 minutes. Add the cumin, chili powder, oregano, and chiles. Stir together. Increase heat to medium high and add the broth, chicken, corn, and beans. Bring to a low boil and let bubble for 20 minutes while flavors meld.

Add the cream cheese and stir to let it melt. Add the crema and stir. Taste and adjust seasonings with salt and additional cumin, chili powder, and oregano if desired. Garnish with toppings of choice.

creamy, cheesy comfort

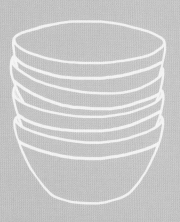

creamy corn and roasted poblano soup

Poblano chiles have a wonderful, deep pepper flavor but hardly any heat if you remove the seeds and ribs after roasting the chiles.

2 poblano chiles
1 tablespoon vegetable oil
1 tablespoon butter
1 small onion, diced
½ red bell pepper, chopped
1 clove garlic, minced

1 (12-ounce) package frozen corn, thawed, or 1 (14.5-ounce) can corn, with liquid
1 (14.5-ounce) can chicken broth
4 ounces cream cheese

1 cup half-and-half
¼ cup chopped fresh cilantro
Salt and pepper
1 scallion, green parts only, chopped, for garnish

Preheat oven to 425 degrees F.

Place the poblanos on a baking sheet and roast in the oven until the skins blister or separate from the flesh. Remove from oven and seal in a plastic bag to continue steaming. When cool, scrape skin from chiles, and remove seeds and ribs; dice.

Heat the oil and butter in a medium saucepan. Sauté the onion, bell pepper, and garlic over medium heat for 5 to 7 minutes, until onion turns translucent. Add the corn, chiles, and broth and bring to a boil. Remove from heat and purée one-third to one-half of the soup, reserving the rest. Add the purée back into the soup along with the cream cheese, half-and-half, and cilantro. Heat through. When hot, taste and adjust seasonings with salt and pepper. Serve with a garnish of scallion.

wild rice and mushroom soup

Umami. Earthy. Begs for a hunk of crusty bread. (TIP: Substituting all wild rice for the full amount of rice blend makes a truly scrumptious soup.)

———— MAKES 6 TO 8 SERVINGS ————

1 cup uncooked wild, brown, and white rice blend

2 teaspoons salt

2 cups cold water

2 slices bacon, chopped

2 tablespoons olive oil

4 tablespoons butter, divided

8–10 ounces baby portabella mushrooms, sliced and chopped

1 leek, chopped (white and tender green parts)

3 tablespoons all-purpose flour

2 (14.5-ounce) cans chicken broth

Juice of $\frac{1}{2}$ lemon

1 cup half-and-half

$\frac{1}{4}$ cup heavy cream

1 tablespoon chopped flat-leaf parsley

$\frac{1}{2}$ teaspoon pepper

1 teaspoon salt

In a large saucepan cook the rice in salted water according to package directions. Meanwhile, cook the bacon in a large frying pan over medium-high heat until it renders some of its fat. Add the oil plus 2 tablespoons of the butter and let heat. Add the mushrooms and sauté with the bacon until mushrooms turn dark and release some of their liquid. (Be careful not to let the bacon burn.) Remove mushrooms and bacon to a bowl and reserve juices in the pan.

Add remaining 2 tablespoons butter and the leek to the pan. Sauté over medium heat for 8 to 12 minutes, until leek wilts. Return mushroom-bacon mixture to pan and sprinkle everything with the flour. Toss and cook for about 2 minutes. Add mushroom-leek mixture to cooked rice; add the broth. Deglaze frying pan with lemon juice and pour that into the rice. Add half-and-half, cream, parsley, pepper, and salt; bring to a boil to heat through. Taste and adjust seasonings.

VARIATION: For Chicken, Rice, and Mushroom Soup, substitute water for the half-and-half and cream. Add 1 cup of diced precooked chicken.

chicken tortellini soup with artichoke and green olives

A surprisingly scrumptious combination of Italian ingredients elevates homemade chicken soup beyond "classic" all the way to supreme!

1 tablespoon olive oil

1/3 cup finely chopped onion

¼ teaspoon garlic powder

4 cups chicken broth

4 cups water

1 tablespoon (or more) Better Than Bouillon chicken base

2 cups diced cooked chicken

1 (14-ounce) can artichoke hearts,* chopped

15–20 pimento-stuffed green olives, sliced

½ cup orzo pasta

4 ounces cheese tortellini

2 tablespoons butter

2 tablespoons all-purpose flour

1 cup cream

Pepper

In a large soup pot, heat the olive oil and sauté the onion until translucent. Add the garlic powder, broth, water, bouillon, chicken, artichokes, and olives. Bring to a boil and add the orzo; cook at a low boil for about 8 minutes, stirring frequently. Add the tortellini and cook for the length of time indicated on package directions, about 8 to 10 minutes.

Meanwhile, make a roux by melting the butter in a small skillet. Mix in the flour, and cook over medium heat until the flour begins to brown, stirring frequently. Let cook on low for 2 to 3 minutes. Add about 1/2 cup of the soup liquid to the roux and stir to combine. Then stir the roux into the soup, mixing well. Stir in the cream. Taste and adjust the flavor base with bouillon if desired, adding 1 teaspoon at a time and tasting. Add pepper to taste.

*Remove any tough, stringy outer leaves.

cream of dilly mushroom soup

Just twenty minutes from start to serve, this mushroom-lovers delight can be eaten as soup or served as a sauce for chicken, steak, or meat loaf.

——— MAKES 4 SERVINGS ———

2 tablespoons olive oil

1 tablespoon butter

1 onion, chopped

8 ounces white or cremini mushrooms, sliced

2 teaspoons dried dill weed

1 (14.5-ounce) can vegetable broth

2 tablespoons sour cream

$\frac{1}{2}$ teaspoon paprika

1 teaspoon seasoned salt

4 tablespoons all-purpose flour

1 cup milk

3 ounces plain yogurt

Salt and pepper

In a medium saucepan, heat the oil and butter. Sauté onion on medium-high heat until it begins to turn translucent. Add the mushrooms and continue cooking until they have turned glossy and slightly brown. Sprinkle with dill weed and cook for 1 minute longer. Stir in the broth, sour cream, paprika, and seasoned salt. Bring to a boil. Whisk the flour into the milk. Add milk and yogurt to the saucepan and return to boiling over medium-high heat, stirring, until soup thickens. Adjust flavor with salt and pepper.

cream of zucchini soup

This pretty soup is an excellent way to use garden zucchini that have grown too big while you had your back turned. No need to scrape out the seeds; they'll turn into purée right along with the rest of the vegetable. This recipe requires balancing the flavor base toward the end: neither the squash nor the salt should take over.

———— MAKES 6 TO 8 SERVINGS ————

2 pounds zucchini, or 1 very large zucchini

1 tablespoon dehydrated chopped onion

1 1/2 cups water

1 teaspoon seasoned salt

1 teaspoon dried dill weed

1 tablespoon chicken bouillon powder or base

1 1/2 cups milk

6 tablespoons butter

6 tablespoons all-purpose flour

Pepper

Trim ends from the zucchini and cut into thick rounds. Place zucchini and onion in a medium-size saucepan with the water, cover pan, and boil until zucchini is tender. Purée zucchini and cooking liquid in a blender until fully liquefied (green flecks will be visible). Return purée to the saucepan and add salt, dill, bouillon, and milk. Reheat on medium, stirring frequently.

In a medium frying pan, make a roux by melting the butter and stirring in the flour. Cook for about 3 minutes to cook the flour. Ladle some of the soup into the roux in small portions and stir together; little by little the roux will absorb the liquid and become creamy. When it is creamy enough to pour or spoon into the saucepan, do so; whisk roux into soup vigorously to prevent flour lumps.

Season to taste with pepper and, if needed, a small amount of bouillon or salt.

VARIATION: For Cream of Spinach Soup, use 1 small zucchini instead of 2 pounds, and add 24 ounces fresh or frozen spinach. Add 1 (15-ounce) can chicken broth when you add the water.

peas and carrots cheese soup

This is truly a bowl of comfort. The recipe is inspired by a yummy cheese soup from a favorite old restaurant, now defunct. I'm pretty sure they used Velveeta instead of cheddar, because their soup base was perfectly smooth.

1 cup (2 sticks) butter
1 cup all-purpose flour
6 cups water
1 onion, finely chopped

3 ribs celery, chopped
2 tablespoons Better Than Bouillon chicken base
24 ounces frozen peas and carrots, thawed

2 cups milk
1 pound medium cheddar cheese, grated
Pepper

In a deep skillet or medium-size pot, melt the butter over medium heat, and then add the flour. Combine well and cook for 5 to 7 minutes, stirring occasionally, to make a roux.

In a separate large pot, add the water, onion, celery, and bouillon. Cover, bring to a boil over medium high, and then reduce heat to maintain a steady low boil. Cook for 20 to 25 minutes, until vegetables are tender. Add the peas and carrots, bring to a boil, cover, and cook for about 5 minutes.

Meanwhile, over medium heat, make a white sauce by adding the milk to the roux 1 cup at a time, whisking thoroughly to blend completely. Then stir in the cheese a little at a time, letting each addition melt before adding more. Stir frequently to prevent burning. The sauce will be thick.

Pour the cheese sauce into the vegetables and stir well to blend sauce with the water. (TIP: Don't let the soup boil after adding the cheese sauce, because cheese will stick to the pan.) Season with pepper and a little more bouillon to taste.

VARIATIONS: For Hearty Vegetable Cheese Soup, add 1 peeled and diced russet potato with the vegetables, and choose a vegetable mix with greater variety, including lima beans.

For Curry Cheese Soup, add 2 to 3 teaspoons curry powder to the cheese sauce.

pimento cheese soup

From friends who live in the South I have learned how Southerners relish their pimento cheese. They eat it on sandwiches, in celery, and on eggs—for starters. When visiting Savannah, I lunched at the Gryphon Tea Room, where I had their famous pimento cheese sandwich. My memory of it was the inspiration for this soup. (TIP: Cook your bacon and make toast points before making the soup.)

───── MAKES 2 PLUS QUARTS ─────

8 carrots, diced

2 cups diced celery

6 cups water

3 tablespoons Better Than Bouillon chicken base

8 ounces diced pimento, with liquid

6 tablespoons mayonnaise

2 teaspoons Worcestershire sauce

4 tablespoons butter

4 tablespoons all-purpose flour

1 pound medium or sharp cheddar cheese, grated

1/2 pound Colby Jack cheese, grated

Pepper

1 cup crumbled crisp bacon, for garnish

Toast points, for serving

In a soup pot, add the carrots, celery, water, and bouillon; bring to a boil over medium-high heat and cook until vegetables are soft. Add pimento. Using a hand-held or stand blender, purée vegetables with their liquid until smooth. Add the mayonnaise and Worcestershire sauce during last minute of blending. (Return soup to pan if you removed it and keep warm on low heat.)

In a medium frying pan, cook butter and flour together to make a roux. Cook until flour begins to turn golden, stirring frequently. Ladle soup liquid into roux in small amounts and mix together to loosen the roux until it is spoonable or pourable. Add roux to soup and whisk thoroughly to break up any lumps. Add all the cheese in three parts, stirring to let each addition melt. Heat through but do not let soup boil, as cheese might stick to the pan. Season to taste with pepper.

Garnish each serving with crumbled bacon, and serve with toast points.

index

Madge Baird is a seasoned cooking and lifestyle book editor and the author of five previous cookbooks, including *How D'ya Like Them Apples, 101 Things to Do With Rotisserie Chicken, 101 Things to Do With Apples,* and *200 Soups.*

METRIC CONVERSION CHART

VOLUME MEASUREMENTS		WEIGHT MEASUREMENTS		TEMPERATURE CONVERSION	
U.S.	METRIC	U.S.	METRIC	FAHRENHEIT	CELSIUS
1 teaspoon	5 ml	1/2 ounce	15 g	250	120
1 tablespoon	15 ml	1 ounce	30 g	300	150
1/4 cup	60 ml	3 ounces	80 g	325	160
1/3 cup	80 ml	4 ounces	115 g	350	175
1/2 cup	125 ml	8 ounces	225 g	375	190
2/3 cup	160 ml	12 ounces	340 g	400	200
3/4 cup	180 ml	1 pound	450 g	425	220
1 cup	250 ml	2 1/4 pounds	1 kg	450	230

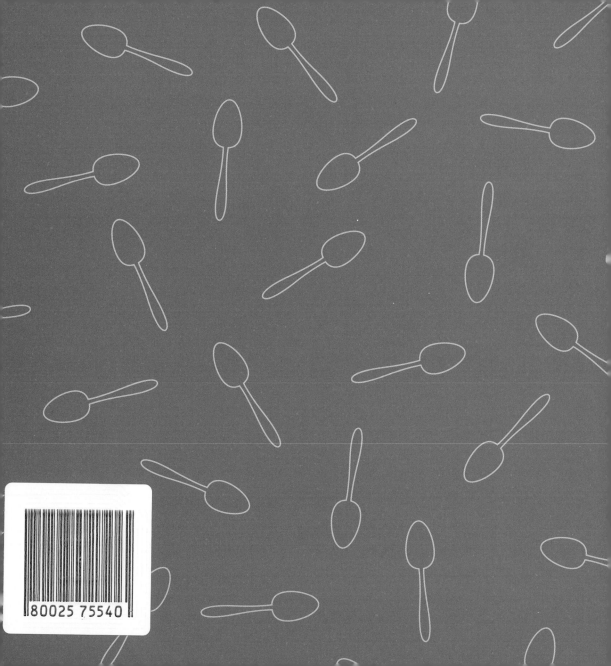

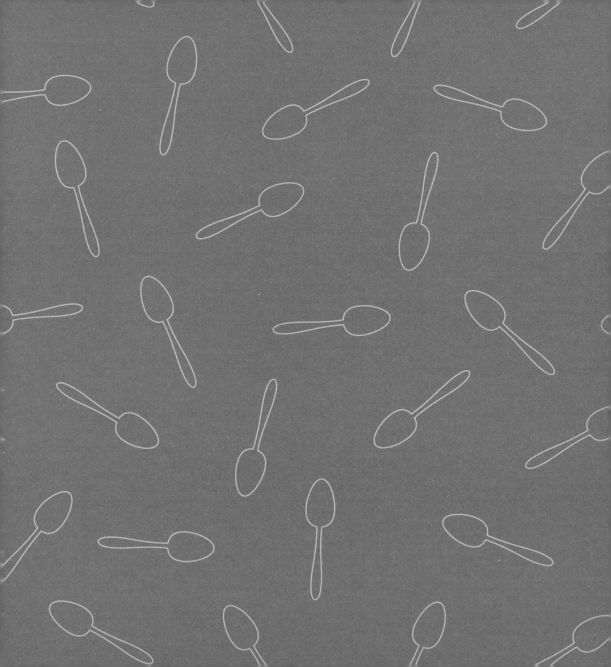